SAND CASTLES DO NOT FALL :

New Holderness Verse

by

GODFREY HOLMES

Godfrey Holmes
Kent 2014

ISBN : 978-0-9536016-4-6

A catalogue record of this collection is available from the British Library

NETHERMOOR BOOKS
Bourne House
35 Tunstall Green
Chesterfield
Derbyshire
S40 2DY
Telephone : 01246-769836

Contact the Author / Photographer :
godfrey.holmes@btinternet.com

Any viewpoint expressed in this Verse is entirely
that of the Author – independent of
St.Patrick's Church Patrington,
its Congregation, the Benefice -
or the Diocese of York

Printed in England by SPIRE GRAPHICS Ltd.,
Bridge Street, Clay Cross, Derbyshire S45 9NU

SANDCASTLES DO NOT FALL

IS DEDICATED TO

GILLIAN PEARL &

DAPHNE CHRISTINE

" *Passing down a lonely street, the Sultan heard
women's voices in loud discussion;
and peeping through a crack in the door,
he saw three sisters, sitting on a sofa in a large hall,
talking in a very lively and earnest manner..."*

[The Arabian Nights]

S U P P L I C A T I O N

Spirit of adventure
Spirit of amazement
Spirit of appreciation
Come to me

Come in the cloud and the sunshine
Come in the thunder and the lightning
Come with the wind and the waves
Come with the mist and the early morning
dew

Come to each mountain-top
The floor of every valley
Come to each wayside castle
Each ruined abbey

Come in all mystery and reverie
All music and all poetry

Come in the twinkling of an eye

Come quickly
For I am ready

****

VERSE TITLES IN ORDER OF APPEARANCE :

Continued...

***

VERSE TITLES IN ALPHABETICAL ORDER
***

1) SANDCASTLES DO NOT FALL

Sandcastles do not fall.
Once they're built, they stay
in our imaginations beyond
the threat of cruel annihilation
beneath the force of an
unrepentant Sea.

We : the builders of sandcastles
might well repent :
We built our sandcastles too far out ;
might well resent
destruction of our noble work ;
might well relent
in our determination
to keep rebuilding, fortifying,
restoring, what was there ;
then clarify what we expect of ourselves;
and what we should let Nature -
hardly talkative,
rarely satisfied,
decide.

Yet we *are* resolute –
all through the hours left at our disposal –
to recreate our Sandcastles
where they were
before the dread tide encroaches ;
before sea-water creeps – or leaps –
to swamp the moats we have so finely engineered.

For *when* our sandcastles
seem to fail :
they are still there
on a Different Shore,
unspoiled,
where
no one - no one force - is able
to damage them further ;
even less able
to wipe them clean
from table overladen
Neptune has outspread.

2) PEOPLE OF THE BEACH

Come to meet each of
the People of the Beach
to teach us the value
of enjoyment without payment -
whose raiment is so different from the suits of
morning, mourning :
streetscape from which each
escapes that each might reach the Beach.

[First] Lavinia (Lavvy for short) building her
sandcastle ;
Silvester (Silva for short) engrossed in his rock-pool ;
Divinia (Divi for short) paddling, erect,
 on the edge of her elected sand-bank ;
Chester (Chezzy for short) climbing big boulders
         ere they become submerged by rapidly
         advancing tide ;
Marjorie (Marge for short) outstretched to soak in
the scorching sun ;
Her son : Samuel (Sam for short) hungrily devouring
his ham sandwich ;
Her Dad : Cuthbert (Bertie for short) vacating his
deckchair [in a hurry]
         ere the Attendant arrives to charge him extra ;
Raymund (Ray for short) ready to pay more than he
should for an ice-cream...
While Myfanwy (Fanny for short) wanders round
aimlessly
         wondering what to do next.

I forgot that next to her was –
 until a few minutes ago –
 Dexter (Dex for short) a scamp
excitedly doing everything he has been told not to !

Now here's a stamp
For the postcard you will write at your leisure -
and with great pleasure -
as one who has just joined –
for good measure -
the People of the Beach.

3) THE YELLOW ROAD

<< Take the Yellow Road
from Seathorne to Sigglesthorne
a*t Crocus time :*
When the first harbingers of Spring rise
cheerfully
to pierce thin layers of ice.

<< Take the Yellow Road
from Seathorne to Sigglesthorne
at daffodil time -
When ten thousand nodding trumpets
bask in watery sunshine.

<< Take the Yellow Road
from Seathorne to Sigglesthorne
a*t tulip time -*
When large, attractive, blooms....
not all of them yellow!
grace wayside tubs and verges.

<< Take the Yellow Road
from Seathorne to Sigglesthorne
a*t dandelion time -*
When weeds....
despised in urban gardens....
boast of progress : abundantly rewarded.

<< Take the Yellow Road
   from Seathorne to Sigglesthorne
   at *rape-seed time* -
   When dazzling fields....
   too dazzling to be true ?
   [for three weeks only....]
   do don their finest garments.

<< Take the Yellow Road
   from Seathorne to Sigglesthorne
   at *primrose time* -
   When this remotest corner of a farmers' empire
   serves to satisfy scorned scholar....
   husband hurt ... alike .

<< Take the Yellow Road
   from Seathorne to Sigglesthorne
   at *laburnum time* -
   When.... responding to the invitation of the lilac
   living opposite :
   this tree celebrates Nature... with finest festoons.

<< Take the Yellow Road
   from Seathorne to Sigglesthorne
   at *celandine time* -
   When shiny, golden, petals
   respond to Midday's brilliance....
   Solomon in all his glory.

<< Take the Yellow Road
from Seathorne to Sigglesthorne
at *gorse time* -
When the prickliest shrubs of scrub-land
compensate tiredest tramp....remotest rambler....
in equal measure.

< In fact : take the Yellow Road
from Seathorne to Sigglesthorne
at *any time.... or Season.... of the year....*
For *who can tell* what abandoned apricot, banana,
plum....
what wizened crab-apple....
might tempt small mammal from the
undergrowth....
[long unregarded, undisturbed]
it knows to be its home ?   >>

4) SPACES TO SPARE ?

I have two hundred'n seventy
At Paragon.
Any advance on tow-seven-o ?
Three hundred'n twenty-five
At St. Stephen's.
Any advance on three-two-five ?
Four, thirty-one at Albion.
Any advance on four-three-one ?
Five-five-five at George Street.
Any advance on five-hundred-and-fifty-five ?
Bidding five-five-five empty lots....
Do I hear six hundred ?
Five hundred and eighty-seven on Anlaby Road !
Any advance on five-eight-seven ?
Going, going.....
Six-hundred-and-sixty six
Hull North !
Any advance on six-six-six ?
Going to that fleet manager over there !
Going , going....

Not going to-day, a Sunday.
That's the problem !
They are not going, and
No one's coming in
To help our City out.

5) JUBILATION

It came upon a June day,
A soon day:
Soon before a *bigger* extravaganza
Extravagant beyond any living person's imagination!
An Ocean to engulf everybody with a receiver:
Submerging lookers – listeners – beneath a deluge of
words
images
memorable memories
so difficult to remember.

Soon before cricket, tennis, football
more cricket
more tennis
more football [were that a possibility]

Bringing out the flag of St. George
to replace a string of bunting:
Red stripes on white linen
mimicking the Summer uniform –
were Summer to arrive –
of little girl heading for school,
her father left behind on couch
not ill -
nor full of sentiment for his little girl
achieving, likewise, little?
        Big, burly men – twice removed -
          achieving a little more
      than has been achieved in the past.

So what score do we give The Town :
our Town
on this universal Day of Jubilation ?
Silver, gold, bronze ?
Three out of ten?
or four?
    Or that honour given the runner who never ran :
wooden spoon , casual mention, consolation prize ?
That athlete cruelly denied space on the podium —
    yet spared the ignominy of defeat ?

***

In the Summer of 2012, there were two important celebrations
almost merging with each other :
the Queen's Diamond Jubilee and the Olympic Games
Wimbledon, the British Open and Cricket filling the space in
between.

6)MASTER : ALL NIGHT WE DID TOIL AND CAUGHT NOTHING

<< Cast your net on the *other* side -
And fish you shall have in abundance :
More than any net can hold ! >>

You toiled all night - and caught nothing ?
Cast your net *on the other side* :
Approach each issue from a different angle -
And solutions you shall have in abundance :
More than any head can hold !

You toiled all night - and caught nothing ?
Cast your net *on the other side* :
Approach each crowd with a different frame of mind -
And followers you shall have in abundance :
More than any arena can hold !

You toiled all night - and caught nothing ?
Cast your net *on the other side* :
Approach each setback expecting a different outcome
And bright torches you shall have in abundance :
More than any hand can hold !

You toiled all night - and caught nothing ?
Cast your net *on the other side* :
Approach Heaven by a different route :
And serenity you shall have in abundance :
Beyond what any Saint can contemplate.

7) CLIMBING ON THE ROCKS MAY BE DANGEROUS

<<*Climbing on the Rocks may be Dangerous*>> :

In his ceaseless search for bread,
A gull might land upon your head !

And — swept to shore by howling gale —
You may be gulped by hungry whale !

And - thinking it is time to eat -
A crab may gobble up your feet !

And, as to Prom-wall you do cling,
Jellyfish your rear might sting !

And as you jump between the boulders,
You may find ten Roman soldiers !

And, falling on to golden sand,
Take, as grapple, bruis-ed hand !

And when you want to go much higher :
Slide not : stoking Scouts' bon-fire !

And if the rocks begin to move :
Be not stuck in slimy groove !

And, wishing you'd brought your dearest friend,
One extra postcard you must send !

And, eyeing up a passing girl,
You might lose your new-found pearl !

And that strange man on rampart sat
Could ask you to retrieve his hat !

And, spotting your slim mobile phone,
A dog might think he's got a bone !

And when it goes aw-full-y dark,
Spring tides may reach their highest mark !

And when you call your Mum for rescue,
She might be filling up at Tesc-oo !

***

Climbing on the Rocks may, indeed, be Dangerous !

8) WITHERNSEA ST. NICHOLAS'

Your aisles exposed to bleakest skies ;
High altar in your graveyard lies.

Your windows now contain no glass ;
And pipers play no more — alas !

Your statues, rudely, have been smashed ;
Your tower, by fiercest tempest, lashed.

Your plaster loosens in the rain ;
The arrow is severed on your vane.

Your nave is littered with dead leaves ;
And pigeons nest beneath your eaves.

Your candles which did burn so bright
No longer even stand upright.

Your organ played at every marriage
Was carted off in tinker's carriage.

Your lectern where so many read
Now boasts a bird without its head.

Your pillars which two Sidesmen hid
Can now be sold for twenty quid.

Your Vicar once so good and holy
Now scours the sea for hake and coley.

Your pews once polished best to pray on
Stand in "The Grouse" to put your tray on.

Your tuneful Choir's new-laundered robes
Now feed the moths in dank wardrobes.

Your bells which tolled in one accord
Have been re-cast - and sent abroad.

So Seventeen-Fifty's dereliction
Returns with Bishop's benediction.

And those oppressed by life's cruel load
Must seek their solace up Hull Road.

***

*In 2011 and 2012, there was a big debate concerning
the future of Withernsea's main Parish Church.
It was decided to hold most services of worship
in the adjoining Parish : St. Matthew's Owthorne.
Many York Diocesan consulatations and a Public
Meeting took place as to the fate of the St.Nicholas
structure : Grade 2*-listed.*

9) THE QUEUE AT ALDI

" This queue, Ma-dam, is far too long :
Waiting an hour's en-tirely wrong !"

" Ma-dam : my grape-fruit's dry inside —
My pears as hard as a fairground ride !"

" Ma-dam : my tomatoes came out squashed —
And those there leeks should have been washed !"

" Ma-dam : I wish to pay by card.
If it's re-fused, I'll ditch the lard !"

" Darling : do you need that Bor-deaux wine :
For Sunday Lunch, juice should be fine !"

" Darling : the yogurt's running over !"
" Then go in haste and pick another !"

" Darling : we've bought too big a cheese...
And these fresh flowers make me sneeze !"

" Darling : Persil's up in price.
Al-di's own make should us suffice."

" Mum : please buy me lots of fizzy !"
" Feeding 10 makes me quite dizzy !"

" Mum : just grab those choc-late bars !"
" I thought you wanted racing cars !"

" Mum : our crisps are nearly finished ;
Last week's treat now much diminished !"

" Cindy : put back that An-gel Cake !
It's not as good as what I bake !"

" Cindy : stop jolting babby's pram !
It's all your fault we've woke up Sam !"

" Cindy : you need an a-larm clock :
It's one-ninety-nine: tick-tock, tick-tock !"

" Mrs ! Please pack things *on the shelf-*
And all those do'nuts harm your health !"

" Next time you shop, it's five pounds off !
"Our linctus soothes that dreadful cough !"

" Doris ! It's your turn at this till !
I've done six hours - and lost the will !"

10) C U T H B E R T   B R O D R I C K

Cuthbert Brodrick is his name,
Withernsea his Station :
Kingston's finest architect
Sensed his destination.

Cuthbert Brodrick built the Queen's :
Withernsea's salvation ?
Soon a Convalescent Home :
Reckitt's great donation.

Cuthbert Brodrick went to Leeds :
Its Town Hall his creation.
Gothic splendour where it counts :
Munic'pal celebration.

Cuthbert Brodrick's Corn Exchange :
A circular formation.
Traders there laid down their sacks :
Fed a population.

Cuthbert Brodrick [still up North]
Built Baths for recreation :
Oriental in their style,
Drawing acclamation.

Cuthbert Brodrick's Grand Hotel :
Huge in elevation.....
Scar-borough's pride; also its joy :
Butlins' speculation ?

Cuthbert Brodrick is his name :
Worth commemoration....
Kingston's finest architect
Gifted to our Nation.

11) SPURN HEAD

Spurn : on your moody mudflats
my cautious feet are welcome ;
Spurn : in your bird-hides
my clumsy feet are *un*welcome ;
Spurn : across your sand-dunes
my shuffling feet are hidden ;
Spurn : up your lighthouse
my eager feet are forbidden ;
Spurn : down your long concrete road
my wandering feet are curiously satisfied ;
Spurn : along your railway-line
my pioneering feet are *dis*satisfied ;
Spurn : behind your war-defences
my pacific feet are curious ;
Spurn : beside your lifeboat
my specific feet are deemed in*ju*rious.

So : when I *return* to Spurn, how will my feet
be *rated* ?
That I do not know, my Friend .....
except they are elated.

12) THE ONE WHO TRAVELLED WITH ME

My Friend is as the River-Bed
Elusive
Seeking not estimation
But that course which -
Though it be least observed in ground undulant -
Gives me nurture.

My Friend is as the Holly-Tree
Corrective
Seeking not adulation
But that name which -
Though it be most obscure in direct'ry corpulent -
Gives me stature.

My Friend is as the Farmyard
Distinctive
Seeking not delectation
But that grind which -
Though it be least cherished in landscape verdant -
Gives me pasture.

And
My Friend is as the Weather-Vane
Instinctive
Seeking not motivation
But that surge which -
Though it be undetected in climate petulant -
Gives me rapture.

13) BARROW BOY BILLY

" Please take my case. I'll pay a shilling....
Next Friday, too, if you are willing ?"

" Boy ! Help me out with all this lumber....
At *Golden Sands* I'll get some slumber !"

" You there ! My jour-ney's been quite awful !
Use that short-cut — if it be lawful."

" Hey, lad ! I like your home-made cart !
Once Fi-do's in, we'll make a start !"

" Thank Goodness, son, you know the way...
Left on my own, I'd take all day !"

" Please buy some sherbets with this note :
I found ten-bob in Gran-dad's coat !"

" O-ver here ! I've brought a trunk :
Weigh's a ton ! You've got some spunk !"

" Why did I come with these six kids ?
To halt their wail, we'll put on skids !"

" How good of you to meet us early !
Your hair's like mine : dark brown and curly."

" She cooks my fish at the *Sunrise* :
Creates a stink ! But what a prize !"

A SIMPLE CHAP :
PLEASE CALL ME BILLY !
TWO BIKES FROM SCRAP :
JOINED BY OUR JILLY !

14) LOST PROPERTY

" I'm asking about a Spire :
Has anyone handed in a Spire ?"

" Hold on a mo !
I'll look in the book.

" Sorry, no Spire down !"

" But that's the point !
Our Spire *is* down !"

" Tell me :
What is your Spire made of ?"

" Wood, lead....
Quite heavy really."

" Age ?"

" Twelfth Century."

" Any distinguishing features ?"

" High : yes, I'd definitely say high....
But not nearly as high as other Spires.
Come to think of it : it does have a piece of metal on
the top
An 'N'."

" Any value ?"

" Priceless really.
You can't get them like that these days."

" So when did you first notice it missing ?"

" When I set off to Church one day, and saw it was not there."

" Gone ?"

" Yes gone completely."

" And you say it was a Sunday ?"

" Yes : a Sunday in 1968 or 1969."

" And what name shall I put down on the page...
In case it's found at any stage ?"

" K ! I mean KEY...: K. INGHAM.
Hold on ! There's someone knocking on the door !
It's our Vicar !
Is it okay if I ring you back in a few years' time ?"

15) LEFT WIDE OPEN

The train passed here : right where I'm standing.
You can see the rails : in road me-and'ring.
City to coast : yes, far-off coast....
yet, in my boyhood, willing host
to wayside farms
which brought their cows, also their lambs,
fresh milk and eggs, jute, beet and yams
for markets : Leicester, Stoke, Bungay,
imag'ning this a *Permanent* Way.
Perm-a-nent not, I'm sore afraid...
Like me, you're abject, quite dismayed !
Yet there *is* hope here, this warm June :
windmills, new plant - instead of ruin.
For petrol products we give thanks :
tubes, stanch'ons, pipes, filters and tanks...
all brightly lit near Paull at night :
in darkness, quite a beauteous sight -
as bright as Cleethorpes' gay arcades,
gracing the Humber's prom-en-ades ;
dwarfed [let no punter turn more sour !]
by neighb'ring Grimsby's gaunt Dock Tower —
where once a year the Port gives you scope
to abseil down, attached to rope.
Your eyes now turn to Bull Sands' Fort :
by Word War's ending sleeping caught.
All round me, too, six stout Church towers
Attesting to the Good Lord's powers :
Hedon, Tunstall, Elstronwick,
Skeffling, Preston, squat Wel'ick.
And when there's nothing else to see :
collect the acorns 'neath yon tree....
and think of Yorkshire with no Beeching,
lessons well learnt without the teaching !

16) WHEN GOSPEL CHOIR TO COUNTRY CHAPEL CAME

And some were sure what they next ought to do ;
And some did merely look to Left or Right
To copy : when unsure what next to mime ;
Or smile : a sweet, seraphic, smile
To please their God -
Or lesser souls to please.

And some in crowded gallery did stand :
For that they felt they really ought to do
In imitation of the choir below ;
While looking to the Left and to the Right
To urge their neighbours - children too -
To stand and whoop and sway :
They *too* intent to please their God ?
Such overdone devotion :
Emotion
Humbler souls disdain.

Black women - fewer white - inspired
Did sing as they had never sung before ;
Danced with a fervour ;
Clapping, cheering, chanting
As clubbers might, until the night is spent :
Gyrations *more* their God to please
Were he a partner seeking joint release.

Or else to win disciples
Not yet won
By brash display, with harmony begun.

17) CLIFF–TOP CAR BOOT SALE

In the far distance
tables are all set
on this, a windswept cliff-top :
host most inhospitable
yet of itself just like a table set
for guests - posh Sunday guests -
expected at Noon...

Only this is not Noon !
It's six in the morning -
most certainly a *Sunday* morning -
when very many people : not posh people...
not posh in the least : these people
are yawning
as... in droves
they turn up to find a bargain :

> a radio without its dial ;
> a horsehair bear which does not smile ;
> a plant-pot offered without seed ;
> electric kettle with no lead ;
> a fishing-rod without its reel ;
> a Dinky-car that's lost its wheel ;
> an anorak stripped of its fleece ;
> a jigsaw missing just one piece ;
> *Cheshire Life* s without their binder ;
> the kitchen clock that needs a winder ;
> a sewing-kit without white cotton ;
> some bags of apples going rotten....

Come and buy !

Last chance to buy
batteries, eight batteries :
"Duracell...
they sell for more !"
"I'll take a quid..."
"Please rid me of these new tree-loppers;
a sequinned dress for weeny-boppers;
a shovel made of gleaming copper;
and vacuum-flask with heat-proof stopper !"

And at the gate -
just where once stood the farmer's churn –
an urn :
a solitary urn
supplying tea and cakes
for all who take
more to their boots
than what they brought with them...
or bought, when off their guard.

18) OUT ON THE LAWN

I hear our Landlord - in his darkest hour ? -
has collapsed.
And lost the confidence of his banker
who has called in all money owed :
from a man who reaped where he had not sowed...

All this *unknown* to his good tenants-
and we are good too- who
uninformed of a saga played out beyond their hearing
[a determination they should *not* hear anything of it]
came back one evening to find their treasured
possessions - and they *were* treasured -
all stacked - crudely stacked - on the lawn
all dampened by this morning's rain : cruel rain
as if to imitate the cruelty, crudity, of the bailiffs : who
feeling nothing, not anything for anybody,
yet feeling more than the coward Landlord who would
not - *dare* not - bring us into his confidence
scattered our belongings to the wind.

Wish that the wind *had* whisked them away
[so useless are they now !]
imitating the uselessness of he who should behind
prison bars - debtors' prison - weep
as we too do weep :
homeless, friendless, bereft of certainty...
save that sure certainty we are locked out from where
we rightly do belong.

And so I look around me now :
at mountain bike - proud mountain bike -
that has o'er hill and dale swept
ahead of competition
eliminating its competitors, indeed...
effortlessly gliding across deep mud,
hard stone, loose shale :
undefeated till broken by that greatest foe of all -
the bailiffs.

And look at the bed and bedding -
too cold and damp for us to use this night:
duvets, blankets, pillows that once
did supply others short of a bed at night.
[The Landlord's joke that we
should sleep beneath the stars to-night].
Would that I could just sleep and not awake -
except to this wireless whose lead might just
stretch to those living next door
who watched the bailiffs at their worst ,
yet failed to call the Police.

All precious things are nought to those excluded :
excluded from the very house which still
could house them now...
were they and we locked in, not out.

Yes : we the Dispossessed will mourn
that which no longer we possess
and scream, scream loud,
until our mothers, fathers too :
[kindred we did leave so long ago]
take us back beneath the roof
which each week *we still shall pay for*
as we each week did faithfully pay the man *and men* -
who stole our futures and our past.

19) THREE   BENCHES

It was on a Summer evening :
at seven, nine, eleven ?
that three women sat on
Hornsea's highest Promenade
gazing out to sea : an eerily tranquil sea.

The first was young :
too young to be so sad ?
Dressed in simple shirt and jeans :
Looking round anxiously
Lest a man - any man - should come
To sit beside her...so ending
her reverie.
" Why look you so intently at the lapping, lisping
waves ?"
I - a woman too - did ask.
" It was a year - a year ago to-day - that they did
come
to take my tiny Tim away :
a bairn just three months old.
" They thought I could not cope :
' I did not place his needs before my own'...they said
' Nor rise in time to feed myself and he...
Nor wash his little head nor wipe his tiny bum' :
A poor Mum me ! Dejected ; he rejected ?"

The second mother :
[was she 40, 45 ?]
sat on a bench most North, past Floral Hall,
mouth quivering, shoulders shiv'ring
[in just one hour 'twill be pithering !]
And, reaching for a tissue, spoke :

" Do *YOU* agree with War :
Iraq, Iran, Ceylon, Sudan ? "
Delayed was my reply :
"Warrior needs War
as Joiner needs Saw."
"My Zac : they brought his body back in sack,
you know. Now GO !

The third woman
had something even grimmer to recall
[were that possible] she newly out of hospital ?
Her boy - though he by then must man have been -
" Unseen did leap into the waves
[much fiercer then]
to save his terrier from the raging surf
[no power on Earth could hold him back !]
for how he loved that dog ...
and could not bear to see his best friend drowned :
except he was not drowned : my Rex.
"My lad did sink instead : worn out in battle
'gainst this Element : a fearsome firmament
Loud calling Ford to meet his Lord !"

Three women lost – their boys lost too - while only the
tide is sure to return

20)CONTRACT WORKER

I am a Contract Worker
Working to a Contract
My Contractor did draw up
[threw up ?]
in alliance with a second Contractor
[also employing Contract Workers].
And a Sub-Contractor
employing his own gang
of sub-contracting workers :

All to fulfil the terms and conditions
of a Main Contractor
drawn into the equation by Civil Servants
served, in turn, by Servants too
who -contracted out -
operate at arm's length :
their strength that they *too* are subject to Contract
which, though it cannot tightened be
[because it must be loose enough a Contract
to loosened be
as need be].

In order better to serve The Main Contractor
and his Sub-Contractors
and potential contractors
who surely would tender for the Contract
were their owners - subcontractors too -
good enough to work on site
completing all works stated in the Contract :
morning, noon and night
[At night to sleep between the covers of a bed
the landlady has contracted to keep open :

warm at morn for Night Shift...
still warm next Dawn
before the Day Shift
goes on site].

And what a sight they are !
Unstated in the Contract.

✱✱✱✱✱✱✱

21) TUNSTALL
ALL SAINTS'

I cannot imagine walking due North
from my Promenade abode :
along sodden sands,
'neath tumbling cliffs,
unless Tunstall All Saints'
was there beyond
where now I am
[past Withernsea's last breakwater].
This fine Church standing slightly inland
from Tunstall's faintly fortified shore :
upstanding enough
not to be ignored
except by Sand-le-Mer's
less anchored
residents
whose caravan stalled
before they reached
its firmly latched door.

22) THE DAY OF HIS BAPTISM

They streamed into Church a little nervously
Looking around as if not to be seen
Except by those who had seen them outside already
[they whom they already knew]
Rather than seeing those they did not know
And probably did not know who was coming
To swell their tiny Congregation

Inside the Church
They sat together
Hoping that each might show to each
What next to do – and how

Inside the Church
They were immediately the subject of great interest
As if they had landed there from another Planet
Which might as well have been the case
So incomprehensible the Psalter
Worse the prayers

Shall we stand ?
Or shall we sit ?
Shall we kneel ?
But not unless the Regulars kneel
Up front in their devotion

That rail's reserved for they and they only
In any case the babby's still on sops
And grizzling
Drawing attention to itself ?

Some type is thick
Some type is thin
And the first hymn
They sang it to a jazzy tune
The sort of tune they thought
A juke-box played
All of 50 years ago

The Baptismal Card also is also full of words
Some in bold
Most left unsaid by us
The Preacher can say those words
After he has preached his Sermon
Probably a very long Sermon
To please the faithful
Who love to hear that sort of thing

All we can bring
Is a babby not yet named
And 50 p. for their Collection.

23) TIGER KIT

Just short of 11
In a deserted shopping centre
On a deserted thoroughfare
In a deserted City
On a deserted Sunday morning
Activity came to a floor that hitherto
Had seen only *in*activity

Slowly - surely - a heavy metal shutter
Was noisily raised
To reveal a whole cornucopia of merchandise
And one merchant [manager ?]
So anxious to chat up his counterpart
A comely merchant selling perfume opposite
That he had to be sure - absolutely sure
She knew the Gig for Monday night

Except she could not sell perfume
As there was nobody to sell the perfume to
That frosty Sunday morning
Would she perhaps like to buy
Some yellow and black leggings ?
Just to cement the friendship you understand
Or next year's Diary
Black and yellow its cover ?

Or wear one of last year's shirts ?
[Those pertaining to a former Team]
She his most valued customer
If only her Perfume Store
Allowed perfumers to dress
In black and yellow
Instead of beige

His first proper customers
Were Dad and lad
Still far outnumbered
By staff all too willing to show them socks
[black and yellow I presume]
With slacks to match
And vest [black & yellow I presume]
With pants to match
Gloves   [black & yellow I presume]
With scarf to match
Half-length jacket [black and yellow I presume]
Umbrella to match
Shorts [black and yellow too]
Are back in stock at 1999 prices
Reduction insisted upon by the Office of Fair Trading
Themselves so often caught napping

In black and yellow pyjamas

24) FOUR MOTORHOMES

One Easter Sunday
Also Easter Monday
[on Easter Tuesday homeward bound]
Four Motorhomes can be found
On Withernsea Promenade in front
Of residents more used to peering out to sea
Without them

The first : a super-duper horsebox
With separate driving-cab
And separate living quarters
Very long it is
Immediately identified by its personal number-plate
T R 2 : The Road To....wherever it happens to land ?
In the event that the eventing horse
Ever wishes to look out to sea himself
His door is cut in two : head and shoulders above

The second : a conventional Ambulance
A thinly-disguised Ambulance
Beneath its thin coat of white paint still labelled
West Yorkshire Health Authority
Commodious this one - but uncomfortable
Suited far more to a man who's fallen off his ladder
A woman who's scalded herself with water far hotter
than anything found in the North Sea - which attracts

A third : the Wyoming - or is it Winnipeg ? -
Camper van
With its stars and stripes
Its swirling red/blue/yellow logo
This once top of its range

Able to cover the whole of Europe
Effortlessly
But now needing effort [such effort]
Swilling/de-scaling/touching-up
Revamping to sample other Yorkshire strands
But not half as much as

The Dormobile
Allegedly owned by "Hippies"
Veteran of many a peace camp
Many a noisy Folk Festival
Many a trip to Rock
Erstwhile home to tree warriors
Eco-champions ?
Dropouts ?
But never dropping out so far that
This iconic vehicle could not
Join her companion vehicles
Free of charge
For this least heralded
Easter Parade

25) DOCK TOWER GRIMSBY

Dock Tower Grimsby
Three hundred feet
High
Now nigh

Dock Tower Grimsby
Thirty foot
Wide
Espied

Dock Tower Grimsby
Steps : four-fifty
In spiral
Inspired

Dock Tower Grimsby
Water guiding
Cranes
No strain

Dock Tower Grimsby
Pow'r releasing
Gates
Most dates

Dock Tower Grimsby
18-52 :
Rising
Upsizing ?

Dock Tower Grimsby
James Wild's
Dream
On stream

Dock Tower Grimsby's
Minaret
Always praying
Never straying

**Dock Tower Grimsby's
Great beacon
Watching, waking
Nor shaking**

**Dock Tower Grimsby's
Silhouette
Our sleeping
Safekeeping**

**Dock Tower Grimsby
Locked
Entry forbidden
Yet not hidden**

Was Grimsby's landmark modelled on Sienna in Italy ?

26) VISIT OF THE GULL

White
wings outstretched
My gull :
Abdul
flew out to sea
Wide wings outstretched

Ollie and Ulley :
Two Gulls
Who seemed
to respond
best at six
obstinately flew
Out of my sight :
swift flight
Perching
on high lamp standard
Just a minute
before leaving
Pier Towers
for the Spurn

Only two gulls to-day :
Ollie and Ulley
Too full
to eat meat
they leave to pester
Gillie and Willy
Dolly and Wally

No casting to the wind : cold fish, cold chips
will bring aviators more to shore

Nor branflake, cornflake, wheatflake
Or cheese-rind, bacon-rind, lime rind :
All declined !

High the gulls rise - and further
In mists invisible
Ollie and Ulley
Abdul, MacNully

Imitating their screech
I call them
Running down the beach
I call them
But they do not come
Will not ? Cannot ? Dare not ?

Poor gulls ? Rich gulls ?
Dependent ? In-de-pendent ?
Entering other people's lives
At their beck'ning - this day of reck'ning ? : *Never*.

27) ART FOR ART'S SAKE ?

Let us with a gladsome mind
Praise all artists and their kind
For their works for aye endure :
ever pleasing, ever sure.

Hockney's paintings of the glade :
trees and skies in light and shade...
His the canvas that endures :
ever pleasing, ever sure.

Larkin's poems : all his Verse :
writ with wit : expressive , terse.
All his stanzas must endure :
ever pleasing, ever sure.

Brontë's books in Scarboro' set :
Wildfell Hall and its recess ...
A life cut short – yet Anne endures
ever pleasing, ever sure.

And on Tunstall's cliff at dawn :
Merid-ian Line by one man drawn °
Storm-tossed boats might now endure :
ever pleasing, ever sure.

So it is with gladsome mind :
Lives enriched ; art redefined.
Yorkshire's greatest aye endure :
ever pleasing, ever sure.

° *John Harrison (1693-1776) of Barrow-upon-Humber*

28) BEREFT

It came upon an August morn
That Mum and she to Hull had gone
And there they shopped till they had done
Myself so reassured.

It came upon an August morn
That lad did take his motor out
And on the roads did show his clout :
Himself still uninsured ?

It came upon an August Noon
That Police did on my doorbell ring :
" They are bad tidings that we bring…"
Spake they with one accord.

" At Hollym Cross there was a smash
Which did your fam-ly's car involve…
'Twil take some weeks for us to solve :
No one from fate inured. "

So now I sit at home bereft :
No spouse or daughter in their chairs…
But matching benches shall be theirs
For local Church procured.

***

*This Poem was written after its Author arrived too early
for Communion and sat in the Churchyard
waiting for the Warden.
On standing up, he noticed that his bench -
and the adjacent one
were dedicated to two people who died on the same day*

29) HOLLYM RACES

Now it's 1856....
and they're coming up to the starting line !
The *first* day of racing at Hollym.

On the Card : The Farmer's Stakes,
Withernsea Handicap,
Later : The Steward's Stakes.

Tomorrow : The Hunter's Stakes,
Holderness Handicap,
Queen's Theatre Stakes.

Sixteen furlongs the course :
Looking down on it
An almost perfect oval.

The going : good to firm ;
To-morrow : good to soft.

To-day : the Grimston Cup
Definitely to be exalted - nor halted.
To-morrow : the Londesboro'.

To-day : our punters number five thousand.
To-morrow in clear sunshine :
six thousand - or more !
Tuppeny, thrupp'ny, fourpenny flutters lay down.
And still the Amateur Hurdles to chance
the day after that.

It feels like the whole of Hull
has caught the Withernsea train
to get here to-day....

while the whole of Withernsea
has caught the Hull train !

And every trader from Hull
is now unpacking his suitcase of goods :
cobs, plates, and shoes ; hats, cheeses, *news.*
Whilst every trader from Withernsea unpacks
his suitcase of fancy goods :
drapes, flags, gems, sweets,
whistles....
A forest of marts
in battling as fierce
as anything anyone will see on the turf.

Now it's 1865....
and they're coming up to the finishing-line !
The *last* day of racing at Hollym.

*****

*Hollym Races partially replaced horse-racing
on Withernsea's beaches, also its Lighthouse Fields.*

*Hollym Gate Station can still be traced -
although it closed on September 1st., 1870 !*

Until 1864, Victoria Dock *was the Hull Terminus for
Withernsea trains.*

30) BLENDED FAMILY

We are a blended family:
I think, a splendid family -
And before May ended
We went to see the Sea.

You see :
Even by the Sea, Hornsea,
We're not at all invisible
[Which some passers-by find risible].

Gemma has Sea in her genes
As without my trip to the Sea -
to make up the numbers on Slough
Sunday School's outing to the Sea -
age 19
she wouldn't be 19 now !

Good Emma followed soon after :
the product of much laughter
at the end of New Year's Eve :
the New Year I shacked up with Eve !

Neither Gemma's nor Emma's Mum put in for them —
But Eve took them on
plus her son : Ron.
Ron's now gone
but left Pete
who made us feel " complete."

Except for Rita who we fostered.
[We thought we'd lost her
when *her* Mum Isabella appeared].

But Rita bounced back
falling out with the fella
her Mam had met on the rebound
at her local sports' ground.

So there's Gemma and Emma,
Peter and Rita,
little Tiana, mixed-race,
[born of Triana, disgraced
but devout Thessalonian]
keepsake of the Cephalonian
holiday I took
to comfort me
when Eve met Steve !

But now I've got Mandy
who's split up from Andy –
and she's brought Devin
and Devin's brother, Kevin.
And she wouldn't relent
….till Phil came as " cement."

31) SCOOTER WITH NO HOOTER

My scooter has no hooter ;
The Prom is very wide ;
Mave's scooter has no hooter -
So we travel side by side !

Towards us comes at speed :
Another
Scooter with no hooter :
The company we need !

Where is poor Ray to-day ?
His scooter has no hooter
And here's his picnic tray !

Alfresco lunch
[A Tesco lunch] ;
We're quite a cosy bunch !

Some folk look down
With hostile frown
When scooters with no hooter
Almost knock them down !

Yet I : no sinner
Will surely be the winner
When each new scooter
without a hooter
Rolls up for Chris'mas dinner !

✳✳✳✳✳✳

32) HULL'S NEW CARD SHOP

To my Mother's Mother on Mother's Day ,
To my Mother's Mother's sister on Mother's Day,
To my Sister-in-Law's Mother-in-Law on Mother's Day,
To my Mother-in-Law's Sister on Mother's Day,
To my Sister's partner's Aunt on Mother's Day,
To my Cousin's partner's Sister on Mother's Day,
To my Cousin's Daughter-in-Law on Mother's Day,
To my Daughter-in-Law's Cousin on Mother's Day,
To my Auntie's Daughter-in-Law on Mother's Day,
To my Son-in-Law's Mother on Mother's Day,
To my Son's Auntie's Mother on Mother's Day,
To my Daughter on Mother's Day,
To my Daughter's Sister-in-Law on Mother's Day,
To my Daugher-in-Law's, Sister-in-Law's Mother on
Mother's Day,
To my Son's partner's Mother on Mother's Day,
To my Son's partner's Aunt on Mother's Day,
To my Son's Sister-in-Law's Mother on Mother's Day,
To my partner's own Mother on Mother's Day,
To my partner's Mother's Sister on Mother's Day,
To my Brother-in-Law's Mother-in-Law on Mother's
Day :
[Heaven's is that ME ?]
To an unknown someone's Mother unknown -
unknowing - on Mothering Sunday
"GET WELL QUICK!"
"CONGRATULATIONS!"
*"WISHING YOU EVERY SUCCESS IN YOUR NEW
VENTURE!"*

33) NOT LEADING - BUT NOT FAR BEHIND

Two Girls : age twelve, thirteen ? deep in conversation
In the gap between two breakwaters ...
And then a little boy : disconsolate now ?
Cupping his little hands in glistening rockpool :
Not leading - but not far behind.

Two young ladies : age sixteen, seventeen ?
deep in study
In the gap between two examinations...
And then a lad - old enough now to shave ! -
Reluctantly memorizing
the Kings and Queen's of England :
Not leading - but not far behind.

Two women : age twenty-four, twenty-five ?
deep in courting
In the gap between Christmas and New Year...
And then one of their sporty exes - in track-suit now -
Trying to engage dancers *en route* to their Gig :
Not leading - but not far behind.

Two mothers : age thirty, thirty-one ? deep in play
In the gap between Nursery and Infants' School...
And then a younger father : quite harassed now ?
Attempting to change his baby's nappy,
cleanse her face and hands :
Not leading - but not far behind.

Two Secretaries : age fifty-nine, sixty ?
deep in paperwork
In the gap between dictation and last post...
And then a much younger P.A., driven now,
Striving to complete Report with many a pie-chart :
Not leading - but not far behind.

Two Pensioners : age seventy-one or -two ?
deep in Scrabble
In the gap between Afternoon Tea and Supper...
And then a Resident more confused, doddering now,
Wanting to wheel wheel-chairs, draw drawers :
Not leading - but not far behind.

Two Hearses : were they eighty-six, seven ?
deep in ceremony
In the gap between Church and Crematorium...
And then an unidentified Mourner, marching now,
Holding handkerchief to moistened eye unfocussed :
Not leading - but not far behind.

34) THE FLAG

It changes month by month : the Flag
on slend'rest pole now hoisted.
Foisted on me by charming neighbour ?
Whose long back-garden
almost meets my own :
two roads in from the Bay.

Some days it is the flag of Wales :
dragons, black hats and daffodils ;
Some days, the emblem of the Scotch :
tartan, haggis, on Cross of white : a botch.
One March, through tight-drawn curtain,
do I espy an *Irish* flag :
shamrock, stout, on tricolour ?

On proudest days : up goes the ensign
of St. George the Bold :
Saint of Soccer, Migrants,
East End cold...[by Jingo !]
And Bingo !
For *to-day* our little town buries
its staunchest champion -
And for this solemnest occasion
my neighbour hoists his finest drape.
Up goes the Skull-and-Crossbones bald :
A jape to make a few folk laugh :
very few !

     Daft as it sounds : my neighbour's most moving
          flutt'ring of a Flag :
          " Pole ! Not Dole !"
          is back :
          The Union Jack !

Deserved ! Reserved
for Liz and Charles and Baby Bea,
Anne, Kate and Edward, Princess P :
On rare occasions now :
fashioned, rationed...
it will appear
for just a score of days
[twenty...that's plenty !]
each year.
Every **year**
I fear.

35) CAUGHT SHORT

It did not catch my attention
Till out of the corner of my eye
A lanky girl past puberty
Placed one long leg over the stile
As if to repeat her feat
In the hurdles on School Sports' Day
Adeptly followed by another shapely leg
Neatly encased in woven stocking black.

The next lady
Older : richer by far
Fumbled in her purse for 5-pee pieces
Tens and twenties
Until she had enough of them
[Rejecting many of them]
To let her safely through.

Soon followed a noble man of the road
Surely entitled to his weekly wash ?
Who shuffled to the side of Exit barrier
That he might *enter* without code
His frame emaciated
After months of begging
In Queen Victoria Square.

Five minutes later
Two agile teenaged lads
Both apprehensive looking round
As if seeking permission
From assembled throng
For any wrong
They too might do
By paying less than thirty
For cubicle not dirty.

The first did run and clear in one
Before the next - perplexed -
Placed both hands firmly on the bar
Crouching as if on the iron railing
Which was not failing
To tame a surging sea
And jumped between those outstretched hands
Kangaroo-like.

Last came a man of little patience
Forty or fifty - but less nifty -
His confident stride
Cruelly halted when his back foot *stuck*
Tripping him - tipping him - into the vestibule
Where dissatisfied with directions
Whose ambiguity left him baffled
Unrelieved he slunk away.
No luck !

36) ALL FOUR

All four bungalows
Paint peeling, fencing down,
But neat, symmetrical, to
astonish passers-by:
This sight so rare in Withernsea.

All four bay-windowed villas
Nineteen-Twenties', Tudor mock,
But built to match each other, and
astonish passers-by:
This sight less rare in Withernsea.

All four wooden chalets
Nineteen-Thirties', asphalt-clad,
Timber treated - not for long ! -
astonish passers-by :
This sight now rare in Withernsea.

All four tenements
So high, imposing,
Each cleverly, *less cleverly*, split into apartments
astonish passers-by :
This sight more rare in Withernsea.

All four holiday-homes
Wedged into Promenade plot
[joins skilfully disguised]
astonish passers-by
This sight once rare in Withernsea.

All four municipal homes
Rectangular, red-brick :
Part of one row uninterrupted
astonish passers-by :
This sight still rare in Withernsea.

All four wattle-and-daubs
of Tudor Kings or lesser serf ?
Rustic-roofed not built to
astonish passers-by :
This sight soon rare in Withernsea.

All four grand balconies
Iron rusting, corners sunk,
Would afford the finest view, to
Astonish passers-by :
This sight too rare in Withernsea.

All four passers-by
Attempting to understand
the complex architecture
of this most contrary town :
Do put your notebooks down !
Your diligence most rare... in Withernsea !

37) C L I F F - T O P
D R A M A

We three - the three of us who are left -
are mystified as to exactly what happened
that scorching June day
we took our picnic up on to the cliffs.

There we began
to eat ham and eggs,
loaf, flan, tomatoes, cheese.
Simple foods these : washed down
with one glass - two ? - of cool white wine.

When...not forewarned, one of our number - sated -
and stiff from squatting
on unkempt turf,
grabbed her walking stick -
a finely carved walking stick -
and rose.

We - *seated in equal discomfort* -
expressed some surprise at her agility
[fragility, as it transpired].

What we had not seen -
but she *had seen*
out of the corner of her eye -
were a brace of seagulls
flying high above our picnic party :
to grab dead fish,
discarded chips
[abandoned on sands
far below ?]

Surely the flight-path of these birds
was born of perfection,
precision,
as if taking part
in the military art of fly-past :
spectacular indeed.

And so the decision
of our friend
to pretend
to shoot them down !

How we chuckled as she "fired" at them - one by one -
as if her stick was *the gun* they dreaded.
How accurately she did copy - faithfully copy -
those wildlife hunters
she had seen on her TV !

And her frantic antics -
more when such swift and graceful gliders - dippers -
appeared to disappear -
were a joy for us, gratefully, to observe.

She circled just as they did !
She ducked and dived just as they did !
Nor hidd was her weapon
[*such a deadly weapon !*]
as she took aim
time and time again.

Until those gulls
chanced to *come inland* again :
so halting our friend's advance towards cliff-edge.

Now *her back was to the sea*
as we three, still seated,
gazed up to the Heavens
where only the sun shone down.

And how she tried
[her back to the distant tide]
to play the clown
in order to *bring them down.*

Then she slipped,
let rip a gasp...
[there were no stakes, no posts, to grasp].

Disorientated,
she staggered five steps - or was it six ? -
and fell *backwards*
over the jagged cliff
in front of us :
her Yell all part of the merriment ?

Until one of our number
rose to lean over the cliff-edge
to see where she was
[perhaps on lower ledge ?]

Nobly the Coastguard - George -
accompanied by Doctor and local bobby -
carried her body off to the morgue :
speculating, idly,
was her *hobby*
the shooting of clay-pigeons ?

And all the time -
in all the blood and sweat and tears that followed -
the only fear of those two gulls
was shortage of prey :
they tempted to say to their young ones
[in squawking jest ?] :
          " *What folk get up to when they're full !* "

****

38) S I N C E

And since our very happy marriage
The Sitting-Room is now our Garage.
And since my wife took up astronomy
The Kitchen no more hosts gastronomy.
And since my girls won handsome bursary
The Dining-Room is now their Nursery.
And since my son gave up religion
Our spacious Loft holds fifty pigeons.
And since laundry task is no futility
The Conservat'ry is now Utility.
And since I took up breeding hounds
Our Bathroom's strictly out-of-bounds.
And since we all have so much lumber
Our Bedroom is not used for slumber.
And since we saved to buy a laptop
The Office is no good as backstop.
And since <<Pot Luck>> became so cool
Our Passage is set up for Pool !

And since Conversion leads to pardon :
Twelve plaster Saints live in our garden.

39) THE SEVENTH WAVE

The First wave is weak, rolling listlessly,
way short of steps linking Prom with Beach.

The Second wave is slightly stronger, lingering longer,
as it laps nonchalantly towards Step One.

The Third wave flatters of deceive :
pretending to have no force
until its due course thrusts it forward
to cover - effortlessly - Step One *and* Step Two.

The Fourth wave comes charging in
making *louder noises* in its pretend fury.
Although this wave bangs and clatters on the Beach,
its reach - its muster - is notably *less than its bluster*.

The Fifth wave is *stupendous* :
angry, broad and fierce.
It crashes over the top of Steps Three and Four,
easily covering steps five, six and seven.

Then - as if called up for reinforcement -
in comes *wave number Six* :
high and mighty -
determined not to be outdone
by any advance
wave Five had begun.

Except : this wave suffers *loss*.
It cannot *toss* the careless lad who is playing chicken
into the swell...
because of backwash :
that phenomenon of counteraction
born of mistiming :
coming in too soon.

The Seventh wave crashes forward with no inhibition:
its reasonable ambition to excel
where waves One and Two,
waves Three, Four, Five, Six
[observed no more]
failed to dwell more than a few seconds
on that flight of steps built as their challenge.

Wave Seven is beautifully carved and curved :
totally unimpeded by the *indecision* of its fellows.
Unquestioned - undeterred - it drowns
Steps Nine, Ten, Eleven !
If railings were *human*, they might have quailed :
inundated - saturated - by these tons of spray.

And what mattered immensely, intensely,
was that little boys scattered
[no longer playing chicken]
confronted with Goliath
at whom, seconds earlier, they had stared
totally unprepared.

40) THE NIGHT OF HER RESCUE

"Hold the fort for I am coming !"
  Boatman signals still.
  Wave your answer back to Coxs'n :
"With your help I will !"

See the Rover now appearing
over land and sea !
If it finds me in the darkness,
it will rescue me !

"Hold the fort for I am coming !"
  Boatman signals still.
  Wave your answer back to Coxs'n :
"With your help I will !"

Though the gale is round me blasting -
over land and sea -
If his clothing suits all weathers,
he might rescue me !

"Hold the fort for I am coming !"
  Boatman signals still.
  Wave your answer back to Coxs'n :
"With your help I will !"

See the search-light of his headlamp
over land and sea !
Though my driver's door won't open,
he might rescue me !

"Hold the fort for I am coming !"
Boatman signals still.
Wave your answer back to Coxs'n :
"With your help I will !"

See him wading round my capsule -
in the land and sea —
When he pulls me through a window,
he might rescue me !

"Hold the fort for I am coming !"
Boatman signals still.
Wave your answer back to Coxs'n :
"With your help I will !"

See us struggling in the tempest -
on the land or sea -
If we crawl a few yards further,
he might rescue me !

"Hold the fort for I am coming !"
Boatman signals still.
Wave your answer back to Coxs'n :
"With your help I will !"

See his Rover disappearing
from the land to sea,
If it shunts a little backwards,
it might rescue me !

"Hold the fort for I am coming !"
Boatman signals still.
Wave your answer back to Coxs'n :
"With your help I will !"

See their Station in the distance :
reached by land and sea !
Through their calling, skills and courage
they have rescued me !

"Hold the fort for I am coming !"
Boatman signals still.
Wave your answer back to Coxs'n :
"With your help I will !"

***

THIS POEM TOO IS A TRUE STORY, INSPIRED BY – AND
EMPLOYING THE RHYTHM OF -AN OLD GOSPEL CHORUS
COMPOSED BY PHILIP PAUL BLISS, SET TO HIS TUNE
ALSO CALLED : HOLD THE FORT.

ON SUNDAY, NOVEMBER 27TH., 2011, DONNA ALLEN WAS DRIVING
TOWARDS KILNSEA FROM SPURN HEAD WHEN HER CAR WAS
TRAPPED BY THE SAME MOUNTAINOUS WAVES
THAT HAD SEVERED THE ROAD.

WITH GREAT PRESENCE OF MIND,
AND ALERTED BY HUMBER VESSEL TRACKING SERVICE,
RNLI SUPERINTENDANT: COXSWAIN DAVE STEENVOORDEN,
NOBLY ASSISTED BY CREWMAN STEVE PURVIS,
EFFECTED DONNA'S RESCUE...EVENTUALLY ...
BY A DARING JAMMING OF HER CAR'S PASSENGER DOOR
AGAINST THE SHIFTING SAND.

HAD THEIR LAND-ROVER'S HEADLAMP NOT SHONE ; HAD THE
RESCUE VEHICLE ITSELF BECOME SUBMERGED, BOTH DONNA AND
HER SAVIOURS COULD HAVE BEEN SWEPT OUT TO SEA.

IN APRIL, 2012, STEENVOORDEN AND PURVIS WERE BOTH
AWARDED THE [PRESTIGIOUS]
RNLI CHAIRMAN'S LETTER OF THANKS.
IN HIS COMMENDATION, LORD BOYCE WROTE :
" THIS WAS A COURAGEOUS ACT CARRIED OUT IN THE FINEST
TRADITION OF THE INSTITUTE."

41) WHEN NOT AT SPURN

When the crowd cries with loud voice
Jostling on the Prom ;
Cars go up and cars go down
Imagined slights cause me to frown
Then do I rejoice...
and turn
to Spurn.

When sharp rain is blown by gale
Whistling on the Prom ;
Umbrellas up, umbrellas down
My hat from dampened forehead blown
Then do I not fail...
to learn
from Spurn.

When of finance I have less
Strolling on the Prom ;
Prices up and prices down
Hunting bargains - like a clown !
Then do I confess :
I'll earn
my Spurn.

When my kin are scattered wide
I, friendless, on the Prom ;
Shutters up and shutters down
Odd Mam still in dressing-gown !
Then do I decide :
I yearn
for Spurn.

42) ON NOT SKATING ON THE PLATFORM

Over Paragon Station's tannoy :

<< You Travellers are advised
not to skate
down any Platform -
lest they get to Brough too early ! >>

<< And You Visitors are ordered
not to skate
down Prison walkways -
cos it makes the Inmates surly ! >>

<< And You Tourists are directed
not to skate
down trawler slipways.
Fisher-men are very burly ! >>

<< You B'lievers are exhorted
not to skate
down sa-cred Transepts.
God is stirred to right-eous wrath ! >>

<< And You Workers are appealed to
not to skate
down fork-truck pathways.
Or be given Canteen broth ! >>

<< And You Mo'trists are commanded
not to skate
down car park driveways.
Nimble cyclists tend to scoff ! >>

<< Now, You Customers are implored
not to skate
down Asda's aisleways :
five thousand cans take lots of stacking ! >>

<< And You Patients are proscribed
not to skate
down Hosp'tal roadways -
if they don't have doctor's backing ! >>

<< And You Pupils are forewarned
not to skate
down our School corridors –
or they'll get an awful whacking ! >>

<< Yet fliers are *encouraged*
athletic'ly to skate
down *airport* runways:
so they will attain
soonest plane ! >>

43) THE CUE TO QUEUE

Small fish with chips : three pounds,50 ;
Small fish, large chips : four pounds,50 ;
Large fish, small chips : five pounds,50 ;
Large fish, large chips : *six* pounds, 50 ;
Large fish, large chips, peas and gravy :
seven pounds, 50 ;
Small fish, large chips, peas, gravy, two jumbo
sausage : *eight* pounds, 50 ;
Large fish, small chips, peas, gravy, sausage *and one
steak pie* : nine pounds 50 ;
No fish, no chips,
No peas, no gravy,
No pies, no sausage,
No salt, no pepper,
No malt vinegar
But cup of tea which we brewed earlier :
That's 50 pee
Plus VAT:
Howzat ?

44) FLAMBOROUGH'S LIGHTHOUSE BEAMS

[AS SEEN FROM WITHERNSEA]

One, two, three, four...
I'll ask no more.
Five, six, seven, eight...
It's getting late !
Nine, ten, eleven, twelve...
I will not delve.
Eighteen, nineteen, twenty...
This is the age of plenty
Thirty-eight, -nine, forty...
He can be so haughty !
Fifty-eight, -nine, sixty...
He calls me " Little Pixy" !
Seventy-eight, -nine, eighty...
This bag is very weighty!
Ninety-eight, -nine, hundred...
I think I am an hungred !

***

ON A CLEAR NIGHT, THE AUTHOR NOTICED HE COULD COUNT TO
FOUR WHILE FLAMBOROUGH'S BEAM WAS ON – THEN COUNT
ANOTHER FOUR...JUST AS SLOWLY...
WHILE FLAMBOROUGH'S BEAM WAS OFF.
DIFFERENTIAL TIMING HELPS SAILORS AT SEA
TO KNOW EXACTLY
WHICH LIGHTHOUSE
THEY ARE PASSING.

45) LOW TIDE

"You cannot go down to the sea to-day-
because it isn't there!"
"It isn't there ?"
"Yes, blown away,
the other day."
"So it isn't there?"
"No : isn't there —
but is somewhere!"
"Near or far ?"
"Beyond that star!"
"And bound to return ?"
"Yes that we learn."
"And not foreseen ?"
"It should have been !"
"When can I bathe ?"
"In next year's wave."

46) JUST US

Just us
On the bus
To Easington ;
Just us
On the bus
To Bridlington ;
Just us
On the bus
To Kilnsea ;
Just us
On the bus
To Skipsea ;
Just us
On the bus
To Welwick, Owstwick,
Burstwick, Withernwick,
Aldbrough, Scarborough.
Except the driver !
She's on the bus too.
She said her name was Beverley...
Or was that where she was going ?
Where *we'll* be heading too ?
When *the boat* comes in :
the boat to Hull
along the River Hull.
Just us
To board...
Except a "Lord" -
by all adored ?
[about to feast ?] :
The ex- M.P.
for Kingston East !

47) WHO'S THERE?

My handset's old :
In fact, it's broke...
My Mam's just met
The weirdest bloke.

So I can't boast
A Smart Phone new...
My bed is damp ;
My pennies few.

And I can't carry
Tablet fine...
My coat's too short ;
The babies whine.

I *don't* possess
An I-Pad dear...
Our front-door's smashed ;
My friends just jeer.

And I can't use
A posh lap-top...
My stomach aches
On crisps and pop.

But every day
I spend three hours
Pretending access
As I cower....

Lest pitying teacher -
Truant bold ? -
Spots useless handset
Very old.

THIS POEM AROSE FROM THE AUTHOR'S
LAZY WALK ALONG HORNSEA'S BEACH.
HE SPOTTED A GIRL CLEARLY DISTESSED -
AND NOT AT ALL WELL-DRESSED -
TEARFULLY TRYING TO BRING HER AGED HANDSET BACK TO LIFE,
UNABLE TO CATCH UP WITH
HER MORE TECHNOLOGICALLY-PRIVILEGED PEERS

48) WAXHOLME ROAD

Marooned upon a windswept cliff :
their backs turned to the sea
unseen ?
A row of twenty cottages :
the biggest "*might-have-been.*"

This might have been a new resort :
of buckets and of spades...
Bright coloured boats launched from a quay :
till latent sunshine fades.

This might have been the meeting-place
For many an artists' school,
A glimpse of vivid canvases
round many a painter's stool.

It might have had a holy shrine
with steps to pulpit high...
A pastor tending to his flock :
God's Kingdom coming nigh ?

It *might have* had a Market Hall
for meat and grain and fish :
Ingredients so whole or rare...
They'd make the finest dish !
It might have had a huge Funfair
of mirrors, dungeons, rides :
With one almighty Dodg'em track
where all the cars collide !

**Instead, this score of cottages
are perched upon a cliff :
each one full-tuned
[with SKY's broad dish]...
*and pond'ring that : " What if ?"***

*One of Waxholme's most famous residents was
Winifred Holtby (1898-1935) :
whose best known book was " South Riding"
and who called Withernsea : " Kiplington."*

49) CROWN ESTATE

Let me take you down to Easington Beach
One Autumn afternoon
Tide's reach...
It is a *Saturday* afternoon

Four ten-year olds
two boys, two girls
appear on the low cliff
with a horse
one rustic horse
one trusty farmyard horse
not a show horse
nor an eventer
not entered for dressage
nor even the local gymkhana

On reaching the sand
a narrow strip of sand
[because of the encroaching tide]
one girl
one rustic girl
one trusted farmyard girl
not a show girl
nor county champion
not entered for trials
nor even the local gymkhana
mounts her horse

Tightening the reins slightly
both horse and rider
gallop a hundred yards towards Spurn
then a hundred yards back

The girl not nervous
[her horse more nervous ?]
straddles the gentle waves
her mount inevitably
causing some disturbance

Sand imprinted beneath his hooves
the horse goes faster
then faster still
yet always controlled
gently controlled
by his young jockey
displaying
skills beyond her age
A perfect bond between mount and rider

Both horse and rider
now retreat inland
to the admiring awe of these three companions
[three children left behind]
I too left behind
in sheer wonderment

50) TWO TROLLEYS;
ONLY ONE BROLLY

In a quiet avenue just off the seafront
two trolleys - supermarket trolleys -
proudly reside in someone else's garden :
the garden of a lady -
not to-day a shopping lady -
nor a shopper *yesterday*,
but probably a shopper
one day in the distant past
[when her ownership of these trolleys :
unashamed ownership -
undisguised ownership -
appeared to have priority
over a shopkeeper's ownership
of the same].

Mum's sturdy boyfriend —
a *semidetached* boyfriend
[to match the structure of his temporary home]
disowns these trolleys,
and dissociates himself
from the act that abducted them
so far from their right home.

Along the Promenade :
two four-year old lads
yearn for pushchairs -
sturdy pushchairs -
that might transport them
even further along the Promenade...

And on that same Promenade :
two Pensioners -
still sturdy Pensioners -
yearn for bath-chairs
that might transport *them*
even further along the Promenade.....

And on that same Promenade :
two widows -
still sturdy widows -
yearn for carriages
that might transport their husbands -
their late husbands -
to the Undertaker residing
even further along the Promenade....

And on that same Promenade :
two teenagers -
increasingly sturdy teenagers -
yearn for *go-karts*
that might transport them
to mates :
daring, sharing, admiring, mates residing
even further along the Promenade...
        BUT NINE INTO TWO WON'T GO !

51) LAST OF THE SUMMER WINE ?

Three Comedians -
three of life's best Comedians -
travel to the bleak, unforgiving, Holderness coast
every Sunday
[every Wednesday *too* in High Season].

Three indulgers of their bus-passes
with three —only three — unvarying routines :
Cafe, Lighthouse, Park ;
Park, Cafe, Lighthouse ;
Lighthouse, Park, Cafe ;
but never Cafe, Park, Lighthouse ;
Park , Lighthouse, Cafe ;
or Lighthouse, Cafe, Park !

And in the Newsagents' -
the all-too-familiar Newsagents' -
all three Comedians exchange jokes
to the detriment of the hapless assistant
attempting to serve some
slightly more affluent customers
patiently in line behind our three Comedians.

Everyone knows them
and greets them when meeting them
knowing their needs
[wants ?] :
pie, carrots mash,
plate of bread-and-butter,
three mugs of tea.

But these are *knowledgeable* Comedians :
more knowledgeable about their Resort
than most of the Resort's own residents !
More knowledgeable about past rail links
than most dedicated railwaymen !
More knowledgeable about politics
than most elected politicians !

And all three Comedians talk to passing children :
asking after their friends, their toys, their hobbies.
And there is nothing wrong or wicked or inappropriate
about these enquiries...
for these are well-meaning men whose only ambition
is to make people - some people very depressed,
distressed - *happier.*
Happier than when they arrived from Hull.
Never dull : these three !
　　[though Hull itself might be dull on Sundays ;
　　　on Wednesdays in High Season].

52) PATRINGTON ST. PATRICK`S

And the little bird said unto the kine :
"Do you see what I see?
Do you see what I see?
A Church ! A Church !
Queen of Holderness,
Set on Meridian's Line,
Along Meridian's Line."

And the little horse said unto the swine :
" Do you see what I see ?
Do you see what I see ?
A Spire ! A Spire !
Ruling Holderness,
Above Horizon's line,
Above Horizon's line."

And the little cat said unto the mouse :
"Do you see what I see ?
Do you see what I see ?
An altar-piece :
Gilt of Holderness,
Most Eastern in God's House,
Most Eastern in God's House."

And the little snake said unto the worm :
" Do you see what I see ?
Do you see what I see ?
Vaulted stone arcades :
Aisles of Holderness,
In Crucifixion's form,
In Crucifixion's form."

And the little girl said unto her Dad :
" Do you see what I see ?
Do you see what I see ?
Much paint-ed glass :
Light of Holderness,
To make we sinners glad,
To make we sinners glad."

And now I say to all ye that pass :
" Do you see what I see ?
Do you see what I see ?
Arch-bishop's gift :
Queen of Holderness,
Now celebrating Mass,
Now celebrating Mass.

VERSE TITLES IN ALPHABETICAL ORDER :

ALL FOUR
ART FOR ART'S SAKE
BARROW BOY BILLY
BEREFT
BLENDED FAMILY
CAUGHT SHORT
CLIFF-TOP CAR BOOT SALE
CLIFF-TOP DRAMA
CLIMBING ON THE ROCKS MAY BE
DANGEROUS
CONTRACT WORKER
CROWN ESTATE
CUTHBERT BRODRICK
DOCK TOWER GRIMSBY
FLAMBOROUGH'S LIGHTHOUSE BEAMS
FOUR MOTORHOMES
HOLLYM RACES
HULL'S NEW CARD SHOP
JUBILATION
JUST US
LAST OF THE SUMMER WINE
LEFT WIDE OPEN
LOST PROPERTY
LOW TIDE
MASTER : ALL NIGHT DID WE TOIL
NOT LEADING - BUT NOT FAR BEHIND

Continued...

ON NOT SKATING ON THE PLATFORM
OUT ON THE LAWN
PATRINGTON ST. PATRICK'S
PEOPLE OF THE BEACH
SANDCASTLES DO NOT FALL
SCOOTER WITH NO HOOTER
SINCE
SPACES TO SPARE
SPURN HEAD
THE CUE TO QUEUE
THE DAY OF HIS BAPTISM
THE FLAG
THE ONE WHO TRAVELLED WITH ME
THE NIGHT OF HER RESCUE
THE SEVENTH WAVE
THE YELLOW ROAD
THREE BENCHES
TIGER KIT
TUNSTALL ALL SAINTS'
TWO TROLLEYS ; ONLY ONE BROLLY
VISIT OF THE GULL
WAXHOLME ROAD
WHEN NOT AT SPURN
WHEN THE GOSPEL CHOIR CAME
WHO'S THERE ?
WITHERNSEA ST.NICHOLAS'

******

ALL SALE RECEIPTS FROM
<< SANDCASTLES DO NOT FALL>>
ARE DONATED TO ST.PATRICK'S, PATRINGTON
IN THEIR ENTIRETY